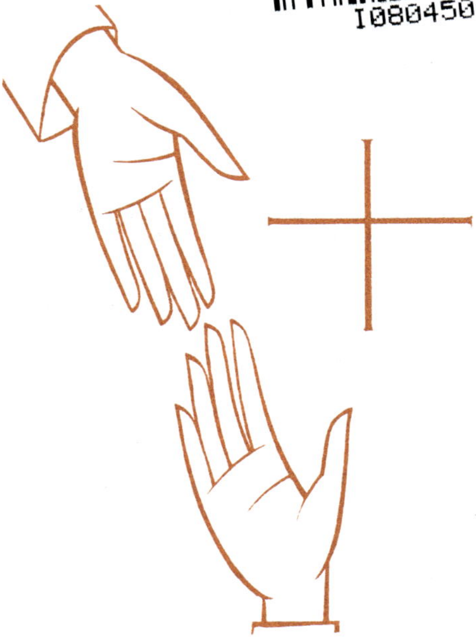

MANUAL FOR THE PENITENT

9 780814 660140

Nihil Obstat:
Daniel V. Flynn, J.C.D.
Censor Librorum

Imprimatur:
+ James P. Mahoney, D.D.
Vicar General, Archdiocese of New York

Design: Frank Kacmarcik, Obl.S.B.

Printed in the United States of America.

ISBN 0-8146-6014-2

PRAYERS OF PREPARATION FOR RECONCILIATION

PRAYER

Lord,
may the Helper, the Spirit who comes from you,
fill our hearts with light
and lead us to all truth
as your Son promised,
for he lives and reigns with you and the Holy Spirit,
one God, for ever and ever.

PRAYER

Lord,
hear the prayers of those who call on you,
forgive the sins of those who confess to you,
and in your merciful love
give us your pardon and your peace.

PRAYER

Lord,
you gave your apostle Peter the keys of the kingdom of heaven,
entrusting him with supreme power to bind and to loose.
By the help of his prayers
free us from the bonds of our sins.

PSALMS: PREPARATION FOR RECONCILIATION

PRAYER FOR GOD'S HELP

PSALM 5:2-6; 7b-9; 13

Hearken to my words, O Lord,
attend to my sighing.
Heed my call for help,
my king and my God!
To you I pray, O Lord;
at dawn you hear my voice;
at dawn I bring my plea expectantly
before you.

For you, O God, delight not in wickedness;
no evil man remains with you;
the arrogant may not stand in your sight.
The bloodthirsty and the deceitful the Lord
abhors.

But I, because of your abundant kindness,
will enter your house;
I will worship at your holy temple
in fear of you, O Lord;
Because of my enemies, guide me in your
justice;
make straight your way before me.

For you, O Lord, bless the just man;
you surround him with the shield of your
good will.

PRAYER OF PRAISE OF CREATION

PSALM 19:8-15

The law of the Lord is perfect,
refreshing the soul;
The decree of the Lord is trustworthy,
giving wisdom to the simple.
The precepts of the Lord are right,
rejoicing the heart;
The command of the Lord is clear,
enlightening the eye;
The fear of the Lord is pure,
enduring forever;
The ordinances of the Lord are true,
all of them just;
They are more precious than gold,
than a heap of purest gold;
Sweeter also than syrup
or honey from the comb.

Though your servant is careful of them,
very diligent in keeping them,
Yet who can detect failings?
Cleanse me from my unknown faults!
From wanton sin especially, restrain your servant;
let it not rule over me.
Then shall I be blameless and innocent
of serious sin.
Let the words of my mouth and the thought of my heart
find favor before you,
O Lord, my rock and my redeemer.

THE GOOD SHEPHERD

PSALM 23

The Lord is my shepherd; I shall not want.
   In verdant pastures he gives me repose;
Beside restful waters he leads me;
   he refreshes my soul.
He guides me in right paths
   for his name's sake.
Even though I walk in the dark valley
   I fear no evil; for you are at my side
With your rod and your staff
   that give me courage.

You spread the table before me
   in the sight of my foes;
You anoint my head with oil;
   my cup overflows.
Only goodness and kindness follow me
   all the days of my life;
And I shall dwell in the house of the Lord
   for years to come.

PRAYER FOR GUIDANCE AND HELP

PSALM 25:1-7; 16-18

To you I lift up my soul.
  O Lord, my God.
In you I trust; let me not be put to shame,
  let not my enemies exult over me.
No one who waits for you shall be put to
    shame;
  those shall be put to shame who
    heedlessly break faith.
Your ways, O Lord, make known to me;
  teach me your paths,
Guide me in your truth and teach me,
  for you are God my savior,
  and for you I wait all the day.
Remember that your compassion, O Lord,
  and your kindness are from of old.
The sins of my youth and my frailties
    remember not;
  in your kindness remember me,
  because of your goodness, O Lord.

Look toward me, and have pity on me,
  for I am alone and afflicted.
Relieve the troubles of my heart,
  and bring me out of my distress.
Put an end to my affliction and my
    suffering,
  and take away all my sins.

A PRAYER FOR HUMILITY

PSALM 86:1; 3-5; 11-13; 16

Incline your ear, O Lord; answer me,
for I am afflicted and poor.
You are my God; have pity on me, O Lord,
for to you I call all the day.
Gladden the soul of your servant,
for to you, O Lord, I lift up my soul;
For you, O Lord, are good and forgiving,
abounding in kindness to all who call
upon you.

Teach me, O Lord, your way
that I may walk in your truth;
direct my heart that it may fear your name.
I will give thanks to you, O Lord my God,
with all my heart,
and I will glorify your name forever.
Great has been your kindness toward me;
you have rescued me from the depths of
the nether world.
Turn toward me, and have pity on me;
give your strength to your servant,
and save the son of your handmaid.

PRAYER OF REPENTANCE

PSALM 51:3-6a; 7-19

Have mercy on me, O God, in your goodness;
in the greatness of your compassion wipe out my offense.
Thoroughly wash me from my guilt
and of my sin cleanse me.

For I acknowledge my offense,
and my sin is before me always:
"Against you only have I sinned,
and done what is evil in your sight"—
Indeed, in guilt was I born,
and in sin my mother conceived me;
Behold, you are pleased with sincerity of heart,
and in my inmost being you teach me wisdom.

Cleanse me of sin with hyssop, that I may be purified;
wash me, and I shall be whiter than snow.
Let me hear the sounds of joy and gladness;
the bones you have crushed shall rejoice.
Turn away your face from my sins,
and blot out all my guilt.

A clean heart create for me, O God,
and a steadfast spirit renew within me.
Cast me not out from your presence,
and your holy spirit take not from me.
Give me back the joy of your salvation,
and a willing spirit sustain in me.

I will teach transgressors your ways,
and sinners shall return to you.
Free me from blood guilt, O God, my
saving God;
then my tongue shall revel in your justice.
O Lord, open my lips,
and my mouth shall proclaim your praise.
For you are not pleased with sacrifices;
should I offer a holocaust, you would not
accept it.
My sacrifice, O God, is a contrite spirit;
a heart contrite and humbled, O God,
you will not spurn.

A PRAYER TO GOD, SEARCHER OF HEARTS

PSALM 139: 1-3; 16-18; 23-24

O Lord, you have probed me and you know
me;
you know when I sit and when I stand;
you understand my thoughts from afar.
My journeys and my rest you scrutinize,
with all my ways you are familiar.

Your eyes have seen my actions;
in your book they are all written;
my days were limited before one of them
existed.
How weighty are your designs, O God;
how vast the sum of them!
Were I to recount them, they would
outnumber the sands;
did I reach the end of them, I should still
be with you.

Probe me, O God, and know my heart;
try me, and know my thoughts;
See if my way is crooked,
and lead me in the way of old.

PRAYER OF A PENITENT

PSALM 143 :1-2; 7-8; 10-11

O Lord, hear my prayer;
hearken to my pleading in your faithfulness;
in your justice answer me.
And enter not into judgment with your servant,
for before you no living man is just.

Hasten to answer me, O Lord,
for my spirit fails me.
Hide not your face from me
lest I become like those who go down into the pit.
At dawn let me hear of your kindness,
for in you I trust.
Show me the way in which I should walk,
for to you I lift up my soul.

Teach me to do your will,
for you are my God.
May your good spirit guide me
on level ground.
For your name's sake, O Lord, preserve me;
in your justice free me from distress.

THE BEATITUDES

How blest are the poor in spirit:
the reign of God is theirs.
Blest too are the sorrowing; they shall
be consoled.
Blest are they who hunger and thirst
for holiness;
they shall have their fill.
Blest are they who show mercy;
mercy shall be theirs.
Blest are the single-hearted
for they shall see God.
Blest too the peacemakers; they
shall be called sons of God.
Blest are those persecuted for holiness'
sake; the reign of God is theirs.
Blest are you when they insult you and
persecute you and utter every kind
of slander against you because of me.
Be glad and rejoice, for your reward
is great in heaven;
they persecuted the prophets before
you in the very same way.

Matthew 5:3 - 12

FORM OF EXAMINATION OF CONSCIENCE

In an examination of conscience, before the sacrament of penance, each individual should ask himself these questions in particular:

1. What is my attitude to the sacrament of penance? Do I sincerely want to be set free from sin, to turn again to God, to begin a new life, and to enter into a deeper friendship with God? Or do I look on it as a burden, to be undertaken as seldom as possible?

2. Did I forget to mention, or deliberately

conceal, any grave sins in past confessions?

3. Did I perform the penance I was given? Did I make reparation for any injury to others? Have I tried to put into practice my resolution to lead a better life in keeping with the Gospel?

Each individual should examine his life in the light of God's word.

I. The Lord says: "You shall love the Lord your God with your whole heart."

1. Is my heart set on God, so that I really love him above all things and am faithful to his commandments, as a son loves his father? Or am I more concerned about the things of this world? Have I a right intention in what I do?

2. God spoke to us in his Son. Is my faith in God firm and secure? Am I wholehearted in accepting the Church's teaching? Have I been careful to grow in my understanding of the faith, to hear God's word, to listen to instructions on the faith, to avoid dangers to faith? Have I been always strong and fearless in professing my faith in God and the Church? Have I been willing to be known as a Christian in private and public life?

3. Have I prayed morning and evening? When I pray, do I really raise my mind and

heart to God or is it a matter of words only? Do I offer God my difficulties, my joys, and my sorrows? Do I turn to God in time of temptation?

4. Have I love and reverence for God's name? Have I offended him in blasphemy, swearing falsely, or taking his name in vain? Have I shown disrespect for the Blessed Virgin Mary and the saints?

5. Do I keep Sundays and feast days holy by taking a full part, with attention and devotion, in the liturgy, and especially in the Mass? Have I fulfilled the precept of annual confession and of communion during the Easter season?

6. Are there false gods that I worship by giving them greater attention and deeper trust than I give to God: money, superstition, spiritism, or other occult practices?

II. The Lord says: "Love one another as I have loved you."

1. Have I a genuine love for my neighbors? Or do I use them for my own ends, or do to them what I would not want done to myself? Have I given grave scandal by my words or actions?

2. In my family life, have I contributed to the well-being and happiness of the rest of

the family by patience and genuine love? Have I been obedient to parents, showing them proper respect and giving them help in their spiritual and material needs? Have I been careful to give a Christian upbringing to my children, and to help them by good example and by exercising authority as a parent? Have I been faithful to my husband (wife) in my heart and in my relations with others?

3. Do I share my possessions with the less fortunate? Do I do my best to help the victims of oppression, misfortune, and poverty? Or do I look down on my neighbor, especially the poor, the sick, the elderly, strangers, and people of other races?

4. Does my life reflect the mission I received in confirmation? Do I share in the apostolic and charitable works of the Church and in the life of my parish? Have I helped to meet the needs of the Church and of the world and prayed for them: for unity in the Church, for the spread of the Gospel among the nations, for peace and justice, etc.?

5. Am I concerned for the good and prosperity of the human community in which I live, or do I spend my life caring only for myself? Do I share to the best of my

ability in the work of promoting justice, morality, harmony, and love in human relations? Have I done my duty as a citizen? Have I paid my taxes?

6. In my work or profession am I just, hard-working, honest, serving society out of love for others? Have I paid a fair wage to my employees? Have I been faithful to my promises and contracts?

7. Have I obeyed legitimate authority and given it due respect?

8. If I am in a position of responsibility or authority, do I use this for my own advantage or for the good of others, in a spirit of service?

9. Have I been truthful and fair, or have I injured others by deceit, calumny, detraction, rash judgment, or violation of a secret?

10. Have I done violence to others by damage to life or limb, reputation, honor, or material possessions? Have I involved them in loss? Have I been responsible for advising an abortion or procuring one? Have I kept up hatred for others? Am I estranged from others through quarrels, enmity, insults, anger? Have I been guilty of refusing to testify to the innocence of another because of selfishness?

11. Have I stolen the property of others? Have I desired it unjustly and inordinately? Have I damaged it? Have I made restitution of other people's property and made good their loss?

12. If I have been injured, have I been ready to make peace for the love of Christ and to forgive, or do I harbor hatred and the desire for revenge?

III. Christ our Lord says: "Be perfect as your Father is perfect."

1. Where is my life really leading me? Is the hope of eternal life my inspiration? Have I tried to grow in the life of the Spirit through prayer, reading the word of God and meditating on it, receiving the sacraments, self-denial? Have I been anxious to control my vices, my bad inclinations and passions, e.g., envy, love of food and drink? Have I been proud and boastful, thinking myself better in the sight of God and despising others as less important than myself? Have I imposed my own will on others, without respecting their freedom and rights?

2. What use have I made of time, of health and strength, of the gifts God has given me to be used like the talents in the Gospel? Do I use them to become more perfect every

day? Or have I been lazy and too much given to leisure?

3. Have I been patient in accepting the sorrows and disappointments of life? How have I performed mortification so as to "fill up what is wanting to the sufferings of Christ"? Have I kept the precept of fasting and abstinence?

4. Have I kept my senses and my whole body pure and chaste as a temple of the Holy Spirit consecrated for resurrection and glory, and as a sign of God's faithful love for men and women, a sign that is seen most perfectly in the sacrament of matrimony? Have I dishonored my body by fornication, impurity, unworthy conversation or thoughts, evil desires, or actions? Have I given in to sensuality? Have I indulged in reading, conversation, shows, and entertainments that offend against Christian and human decency? Have I encouraged others to sin by my own failure to maintain these standards? Have I been faithful to the moral law in my married life?

5. Have I gone against my conscience out of fear or hypocrisy?

6. Have I always tried to act in the true freedom of the sons of God according to the law of the Spirit, or am I the slave of forces within me?

RITE FOR RECONCILIATION OF INDIVIDUAL PENITENTS

TEXTS FOR THE PENITENT

The penitent should prepare for the celebration of the sacrament by prayer, reading of Scripture, and silent reflection. The penitent should think over and should regret all sins since the last celebration of the sacrament.

RECEPTION OF THE PENITENT

The penitent enters the confessional or other place set aside for the celebration of the sacrament of penance. After the welcoming of the priest, the penitent makes the sign of the cross saying:

In the name of the Father, and of the Son, and of the Holy Spirit. Amen.

The penitent is invited to have trust in God and replies:

Amen.

READING OF THE WORD OF GOD

The penitent then listens to a text of Scripture which tells about God's mercy and calls men to conversion.

1. Isaiah 53:4-6

Let us look on Jesus
who suffered to save us
and rose again for our justification.

Yet it was our infirmities that he bore,
our sufferings that he endured,
While we thought of him as stricken,
as one smitten by God and afflicted.
But he was pierced for our offenses,
crushed for our sins,
Upon him was the chastisement that makes
us whole,
by his stripes we were healed.
We had all gone astray like sheep,
each following his own way;
But the Lord laid upon him
the guilt of us all.

2. Ezekiel 11:19-20

Let us listen to the Lord as he speaks to us:
I will give them a new heart and put a new spirit within them; I will remove the stony

heart from their bodies, and replace it with a natural heart, so that they will live according to my statutes, and observe and carry out my ordinances; thus they shall be my people and I will be their God.

3. Matthew 6:14-15

Let us listen to the Lord as he speaks to us: If you forgive the faults of others, your heavenly Father will forgive you yours. If you do not forgive others, neither will your Father forgive you.

4. Mark 1:14-15

After John's arrest, Jesus appeared in Galilee proclaiming the good news of God: "This is the time of fulfillment. The reign of God is at hand! Reform your lives and believe in the gospel!"

5. Luke 6:31-38

Let us listen to the Lord as he speaks to us: Do to others what you would have them do to you. If you love those who love you, what credit is that to you? Even sinners love those who love them. If you do good to those who do good to you, how can you claim any credit? Sinners do as much. If you lend to those from whom you expect repayment, what merit is there in it for you? Even sinners lend to sinners, expecting to be repaid in full.

Love your enemy and do good; lend without expecting repayment. Then will your recompense be great. You will rightly be called sons of the Most High, since he himself is good to the ungrateful and the wicked.

Be compassionate, as your Father is compassionate. Do not judge, and you will not be judged. Do not condemn, and you will not be condemned. Pardon, and you shall be pardoned. Give, and it shall be given to you. Good measure pressed down, shaken together, running over, will they pour into the fold of your garment. For the measure you measure with will be measured back to you.

6. Luke 15:1-7

The tax collectors and sinners were all gathering around to hear him, at which the Pharisees and the scribes murmured, "This man welcomes sinners and eats with them." Then he addressed this parable to them:

"Who among you, if he has a hundred sheep and loses one of them, does not leave the ninety-nine in the wasteland and follow the lost one until he finds it? And when he finds it, he puts it on his shoulders in jubilation. Once arrived home, he invites friends and neighbors in and says to them, 'Rejoice with me because I have found my lost sheep.'

I tell you, there will likewise be more joy in heaven over one repentant sinner than over ninety-nine righteous people who have no need to repent."

7. John 20:19-23

On the evening of that first day of the week, even though the disciples had locked the doors of the place where they were for fear of the Jews, Jesus came and stood before them. "Peace be with you," he said. When he had said this, he showed them his hands and his side. At the sight of the Lord the disciples rejoiced. "Peace be with you," he said again.

"As the Father has sent me,
so I send you."

Then he breathed on them and said:

"Receive the Holy Spirit.
If you forgive men's sins,
they are forgiven them;
if you hold them bound,
they are held bound."

8. Romans 5:8 - 9

It is precisely in this that God proves his love for us: that while we were still sinners, Christ died for us. Now that we have been justified by his blood, it is all the more certain that we shall be saved by him from God's wrath.

9. Ephesians 5:1-2

Be imitators of God as his dear children.

Follow the way of love, even as Christ loved you. He gave himself for us as an offering to God, a gift of pleasing fragrance.

10. Colossians 1:12-14

Give thanks to the Father for having made you worthy to share the lot of the saints in light. He rescued us from the power of darkness and brought us into the kingdom of his beloved Son. Through him we have redemption, the forgiveness of our sins.

11. Colossians 3:8-10, 12-17

You must put that aside now: all the anger and quick temper, malice, the insults, the foul language. Stop lying to one another. What you have done is put aside your old self with its past deeds and put on a new man, one who grows in knowledge as he is formed anew in the image of his Creator. Because you are God's chosen ones, holy and beloved, clothe yourselves with heartfelt mercy, with kindness, humility, meekness, and patience. Bear with one another; forgive whatever grievances you have against one another. Forgive as the Lord has forgiven you. Over all these virtues put on love, which binds the rest together and makes them perfect. Christ's peace must reign in your hearts, since as members of the one body you have been called to that peace. Dedicate yourselves to thankfulness. Let the word of Christ, rich as it is, dwell in you. In wisdom made perfect, instruct and admonish one another. Sing gratefully to God from your hearts in psalms, hymns, and inspired songs. Whatever you do, whether in speech or in action, do it in the name of the Lord Jesus. Give thanks to God the Father through him.

12. 1 John 1:6-7, 9

If we say, "We have fellowship with him,"
while continuing to walk in darkness,
we are liars and do not act in truth.
But if we walk in light,
as he is in the light,
we have fellowship with one another,
and the blood of his Son Jesus cleanses us
from all sin.
But if we acknowledge our sins,
he who is just can be trusted
to forgive our sins
and cleanse us from every wrong.

CONFESSION OF SINS AND ACCEPTANCE OF SATISFACTION

The penitent speaks to the priest in a normal, conversational fashion. The penitent tells when he or she last celebrated the sacrament and then confesses his or her sins. The penitent then listens to any advice the priest may give and accepts the satisfaction from the priest. The penitent should ask any appropriate questions.

PRAYER OF THE PENITENT AND ABSOLUTION

PRAYER

Before the absolution is given, the penitent expresses sorrow for sins in these of similar words:

My God,
I am sorry for my sins with all my heart.
In choosing to do wrong
and failing to do good,
I have sinned against you
whom I should love above all things.
I firmly intend, with your help,
to do penance,
to sin no more,
and to avoid whatever leads me to sin.
Our Savior Jesus Christ
suffered and died for us.
In his name, my God, have mercy.

Or:

Lord Jesus, Son of God,
have mercy on me, a sinner.

Or Psalm 25: 6-7:

Remember, Lord, your compassion and mercy you showed long ago.
Do not recall the sins and failings of my youth.
In your mercy remember me, Lord, because of your goodness.

Or Psalm 51: 4-5:

Wash me from my guilt
and cleanse me of my sin.
I acknowledge my offense;
my sin is before me always.

Or Luke 15:18, 18: 13:

Father, I have sinned against you
and am not worthy to be called
your son.
Be merciful to me, a sinner.

Or:

Father of mercy,
like the prodigal son
I return to you and say:
"I have sinned against you
and am no longer worthy to be called
your son."
Christ Jesus, Savior of the world,
I pray with the repentant thief
to whom you promised Paradise:
"Lord, remember me in your kingdom."
Holy Spirit, fountain of love,
I call on you with trust:
"Purify my heart,
and help me to walk as a child of light."

Or:

Lord Jesus,
you opened the eyes of the blind,
healed the sick,
forgave the sinful woman,

and after Peter's denial confirmed him
in your love.
Listen to my prayer:
forgive all my sins,
renew your love in my heart,
help me to live in perfect unity with my
fellow Christians
that I may proclaim your saving power to
all the world.

Or:
Lord Jesus,
you chose to be called the friend of sinners.
By your saving death and resurrection
free me from my sins.
May your peace take root in my heart
and bring forth a harvest
of love, holiness, and truth.

Or:
Lord Jesus Christ,
you are the Lamb of God;
you take away the sins of the world.
Through the grace of the Holy Spirit
restore me to friendship with your Father,
cleanse me from every stain of sin
in the blood you shed for me,
and raise me to new life
for the glory of your name.

Or:
Lord God,
in your goodness have mercy on me:

do not look on my sins,
but take away all my guilt.
Create in me a clean heart
and renew within me an upright spirit.

ABSOLUTION

If the penitent is not kneeling, he or she bows his or her head as the priest extends his hands (or at least extends his right hand).

God, the Father of mercies,
through the death and resurrection of
his Son
has reconciled the world to himself
and sent the Holy Spirit among us
for the forgiveness of sins;
through the ministry of the Church
may God give you pardon and peace,
and I absolve you from your sins
in the name of the Father, and of the Son, ✠
and of the Holy Spirit.
The penitent replies: **Amen.**

PROCLAMATION OF PRAISE OF GOD AND DISMISSAL

Penitent and priest give praise to God:
Priest: Give thanks to the Lord, for he
is good.
Penitent: **His mercy endures for ever.**
Then the penitent is dismissed by the priest.

PRAYERS OF THANKSGIVING FOR RECONCILIATION

PRAYER

Lord God,
creator and ruler of your kingdom of light,
in your great love for this world
you gave up your only Son
for our salvation.
His cross has redeemed us,
his death has given us life,
his resurrection has raised us to glory.
Through him we ask you
to be always present among your family.
Teach us to be reverent in the presence
of your glory;
fill our hearts with faith,
our days with good works,
our lives with your love;
may your truth be on our lips
and your wisdom in all our actions,
that we may receive the reward of
everlasting life.

We ask this through Christ our Lord.
Amen.

PRAYER

Lord Jesus Christ,
your loving forgiveness knows no limits.
You took our human nature
to give us an example of humility
and to make us faithful in every trial.
May we never lose the gifts you have
given us,
but if we fall into sin
lift us up by your gift of repentance,
for you live and reign for ever and ever.
Amen.

PRAYER

Father of mercy,
you always answer your people in
their sufferings.
We thank you for your kindness
and ask you to free us from all evil,
that we may serve you in happiness
all our days.

PRAYER

Father,
you made us in your own image
and your Son accepted death for
our salvation.
Help us to keep watch in prayer at all times.
May we be free from sin when we leave
this world
and rejoice in peace with you for ever.

PSALMS AND HYMNS OF PRAISE AND THANKSGIVING FOR RECONCILIATION

THANKSGIVING FOR THE REMISSION OF SIN

PSALM 32: 1-5; 7; 11

Happy is he whose fault is taken away,
whose sin is covered.
Happy the man to whom the Lord imputes not guilt,
in whose spirit there is no guile.

As long as I would not speak, my bones wasted away
with my groaning all the day,
For day and night your hand was heavy upon me;
my strength was dried up as by the heat of summer.
Then I acknowledged my sin to you,
my guilt I covered not.
I said, "I confess my faults to the Lord,"
and you took away the guilt of my sin.
You are my shelter; from distress you will preserve me;
with glad cries of freedom you will ring me round.

Be glad in the Lord and rejoice, you just;
exult, all you upright of heart.

A PRAYER OF LONGING FOR GOD

PSALM 63:2-9

O God, you are my God whom I seek;
for you my flesh pines and my soul thirsts
like the earth, parched, lifeless and
without water.
Thus have I gazed toward you in the
sanctuary
to see your power and your glory,
For your kindness is a greater good than life;
my lips shall glorify you.

Thus will I bless you while I live;
lifting up my hands, I will call upon
your name.
As with the riches of a banquet shall my
soul be satisfied,
and with exultant lips my mouth shall
praise you.
I will remember you upon my couch,
and through the night-watches I will
meditate on you:
That you are my help,
and in the shadow of your wings I shout
for joy.
My soul clings fast to you;
your right hand upholds me.

PRAYER FOR UNION WITH GOD

PSALM 84:2-4; 11-13

How lovely is your dwelling place,
O Lord of hosts!
My soul yearns and pines
for the courts of the Lord.
My heart and my flesh
cry out for the living God.
Even the sparrow finds a home,
and the swallow a nest
in which she puts her young—
Your altars, O Lord of hosts,
my king and my God!

I had rather one day in your courts
than a thousand elsewhere;
I had rather lie at the threshold of the house
of my God
than dwell in the tents of the wicked.
For a sun and a shield is the Lord God;
grace and glory he bestows;
The Lord withholds no good thing
from those who walk in sincerity.
O Lord of hosts,
happy the men who trust in you!

A PRAYER FOR THE LORD'S PROTECTION

PSALM 90:1-2; 12-17

O Lord, you have been our refuge
through all generations.
Before the mountains were begotten
and earth and the world were
brought forth,
from everlasting to everlasting
you are God.

Teach us to number our days aright,
that we may gain wisdom of heart.
Return, O Lord! How long?
Have pity on your servants!
Fill us at daybreak with your kindness,
that we may shout for joy and gladness
all our days.
Make us glad, for the days when you
afflicted us,
for the years when we saw evil.
Let your work be seen by your servants
and your glory by their children;
And may the gracious care of the Lord
our God be ours;
prosper the work of our hands for us!
[Prosper the work of our hands!]

PRAYER OF PRAISE FOR GOD'S TENDER COMPASSION

PSALM 103: 1-5; 8; 11-12

Bless the Lord, O my soul;
  and all my being, bless his holy name.
Bless the Lord, O my soul,
  and forget not all his benefits;
He pardons all your iniquities,
  he heals all your ills.
He redeems your life from destruction,
  he crowns you with kindness and
    compassion,
He fills your lifetime with good;
  your youth is renewed like the eagle's.

Merciful and gracious is the Lord,
  slow to anger and abounding in kindness:
For as heavens are high above the earth,
  so surpassing is his kindness toward
    those who fear him.
As far as the east is from the west,
  so far has he put our transgressions
    from us.

A SONG OF PRAISE FOR GOD'S GOODNESS

PSALM 111

I will give thanks to the Lord with all
my heart
in the company and assembly of the just.
Great are the works of the Lord,
exquisite in all their delights.
Majesty and glory are his work,
and his justice endures forever.
He has won renown for his wondrous
deeds;
gracious and merciful is the Lord.
He has given food to those who fear him;
he will forever be mindful of his
covenant.
He has made known to his people the power
of his works,
giving them the inheritance of the
nations.
The works of his hands are faithful and just;
sure are all his precepts.
Reliable forever and ever,
wrought in truth and equity.
He has sent deliverance to his people;
he has ratified his covenant forever;
holy and awesome is his name.
The fear of the Lord is the beginning
of wisdom;
prudent are all who live by it.
His praise endures forever.

A PRAYER OF THANKSGIVING

PSALM 118: 1; 4-9; 13-14; 29

Give thanks to the Lord, for he is good,
for his mercy endures forever.
Let those who fear the Lord say,
"His mercy endures forever."

In my straits I called upon the Lord;
the Lord answered me and set me free.
The Lord is with me; I fear not;
what can man do against me?
The Lord is with me to help me,
and I shall look down upon my foes.
It is better to take refuge in the Lord
than to trust in man.
It is better to take refuge in the Lord
than to trust in princes.

I was hard pressed and was falling,
but the Lord helped me.
My strength and my courage is the Lord
and he has been my savior.

Give thanks to the Lord, for he is good;
for his kindness endures forever.

A HYMN OF THANKSGIVING

CANTICLE OF MARY (MAGNIFICAT)

My soul proclaims the greatness of
the Lord,
my spirit rejoices in God my Savior
for he has looked with favor on his
lowly servant.

From this day all generations will call
me blessed:
the Almighty has done great things for me,
and holy is his Name.

He has mercy on those who fear him
in every generation.

He has shown the strength of his arm,
he has scattered the proud in their conceit.

He has cast down the mighty from their
thrones,
and has lifted up the lowly.

He has filled the hungry with good things,
and the rich he has sent away empty.

He has come to the help of his servant Israel
for he has remembered his promise of
mercy,
the promise he made to our fathers,
to Abraham and his children for ever.

Luke 1:46 - 55

RITE FOR RECONCILIATION OF SEVERAL PENITENTS WITH INDIVIDUAL CONFESSION AND ABSOLUTION

Text for people's participation

INTRODUCTORY RITES

SONG

When the faithful have assembled, they may sing a psalm, antiphon, or other appropriate song while the priest is entering the church, for example:

Hear us, Lord,
for you are merciful and kind.
In your great compassion,
look on us with love.

Or:

Let us come with confidence before
the throne of grace
to receive God's mercy,
and we shall find pardon and strength
in our time of need.

GREETING

The priest then greets the congregation:
Grace, mercy, and peace be with you
from God the Father
and Christ Jesus our Savior.
℟. **And also with you.**

Or:
Grace and peace be with you
from God the Father
and from Jesus Christ
who loved us
and washed away our sins in his blood.
℟. **And also with you.**

Or:
Grace, mercy, and peace
from God the Father and Jesus Christ the Son
be with you in truth and love.
℟. **Amen.**

Or:
May God open your hearts to his law
and give you peace;
may he answer your prayers
and restore you to friendship.
℟. **Amen.**

Or:

Grace and peace be with you
from God our Father
and from the Lord Jesus Christ
who laid down his life for our sins.
℟. **Glory to him for ever. Amen.**

Then the priest or another minister speaks briefly about the importance and purpose of the celebration and the order of the service.

OPENING PRAYER

The priest invites all to pray, using these or similar words:

Brothers and sisters, God calls us to
conversion;
let us therefore ask him for the grace of
sincere repentance.

All pray in silence for a brief period. Then the priest sings or says the prayer at the end of which the people answer: **Amen.**

CELEBRATION OF THE WORD OF GOD

The celebration of the word follows, after which the homily is given. If there are several readings a psalm or other appropriate song or even a period of silence should intervene between them, so that everyone may understand the word of God more deeply and give it his heart-felt assent.

Homily

The homily which follows should lead the penitents to examine their consciences and renew their lives.

Examination of Conscience

A period of time may be spent in making an examination of conscience and in arousing true sorrow for sins.

RITE OF RECONCILIATION

GENERAL CONFESSION OF SINS

The deacon or another minister invites all to kneel or bow, and to join in saying a general formula for confession (for example, **I confess to almighty God**). Then they stand and say a litany or sing an appropriate song. The deacon or minister offers various litany formulas, to each of which the people answer with an appropriate response indicated by the minister.

The priest invites all to pray to God the Father.

All say together:

Our Father. . . .

The priest concludes with a prayer at the end of which the people answer: **Amen.**

INDIVIDUAL CONFESSION AND ABSOLUTION

Then the penitents go to the priests designated for individual confession, and confess their sins. Each one receives and accepts a fitting act of satisfaction and is absolved. After hearing the confession and offering suitable counsel, the priest extends his hands over the penitent's head (or at least extends his right hand) and gives absolution. Everything else which is customary in individual confession is omitted.

God, the Father of mercies,
through the death and resurection of his Son
has reconciled the world to himself
and sent the Holy Spirit among us
for the forgiveness of sins;
through the ministry of the Church
may God give you pardon and peace,
and I absolve you from your sins
in the name of the Father, and of the Son, ✠
and of the Holy Spirit,
The penitent answers: **Amen.**

PROCLAMATION OF PRAISE

When the individual confessions have been completed, the other priests stand near the one who is presiding over the celebration. The latter invites all present to offer thanks and encourages them to do good works which will proclaim the grace of repentance in the life of the entire community and each of its members. It is fitting for all to sing a psalm or hymn or to say a litany in acknowledgement of God's power and mercy, for example, the canticle of Mary (Luke 1:46:55), or Psalm 136: 1-9, 13-14, 16, 25-26 or another psalm.

The responses to the various proclamations from

the Scripture are as follows:

Psalm 2: 1-7, 10-11

℟. **Rejoice in the Lord and sing for joy, friends of God.**

Psalm 98: 1-9

℟. **The Lord has remembered his mercy.**

Psalm 100: 2-5

℟. **The Lord is loving and kind: his mercy is for ever.**

Psalm 119: 1, 10-13, 15-16, 18, 33, 105, 169, 170, 174-175

℟. **Blessed are you, Lord; teach me your decrees.**

Psalm 103: 1-4, 8-18

℟. **The mercy of the Lord is from everlasting to everlasting on those who revere him.**

Psalm 145: 1-21

℟. **Day after day, I will bless you, Lord: I will praise your name for ever.**

Psalm 146: 2-10

℟. **I will sing to my God all the days of my life.**

Isaiah 12: 1b-6

℟. **Praise the Lord and call upon his name.**

Isaiah 61: 10-11

℟. **My Spirit rejoices in God.**

Jeremiah 31: 10-14

℟. **The Lord has redeemed his people.**

Daniel 3: 52-57

℟. **Bless the Lord, all the works of his hand: praise and glorify him for ever.**

Luke 1: 46-55

℟. **The Lord has remembered his mercy.**

Ephesians 1: 3-10

℟. **Blessed be God who chose us in Christ.**

Revelation 15: 3-4

℟. **Great and wonderful are all your works, Lord**

CONCLUDING PRAYER OF THANKSGIVING

After the song of praise or the litany, the priest concludes the common prayer, at the end of which the people answer: **Amen.**

CONCLUDING RITE

Then the priest blesses all present. At the end of each petition, the people answer: **Amen.**

The priest may use other forms of blessing, to which the people answer: **Amen.**

The deacon or other minister or the priest himself dismisses the assembly:

The Lord has freed you from your sins.
Go in peace.

All answer: **Thanks be to God.**

Any other appropriate form may be used.